WAR MACHINES
ARTILLERY

Simon Adams

A+
Smart Apple Media

IN ASSOCIATION WITH

IMPERIAL WAR
MUSEUM

Smart Apple Media is published by Black Rabbit Books
P.O. Box 3263, Mankato, Minnesota 56002

Printed in the United States

Published by arrangement with the Watts Publishing Group Ltd, London.

Library of Congress Cataloging-in-Publication Data
Adams, Simon.
    Artillery / Simon Adams.
    p. cm.—(Smart Apple Media. War machines)
    Includes index.
    Summary: "Describes several models of guns and howizters used in World War I and World War II, including specifications and statistics"— Provided by publisher.
    ISBN 978-1-59920-226-6
    1. Ordnance—Juvenile literature. 2. Artillery—Juvenile literature. I. Title.
UF560.A23 2009
623.4'109041—dc22

                                        2007045460

A note on sources used for this book: The specifications and statistics in this book are compiled from various sources and amended to include information held by the Imperial War Museum.

Editor: Sarah Ridley
Editor-in-chief: John Miles
Designer: Jason Billin
Art director: Jonathan Hair

Picture credits: All images copyright © Imperial War Museum. Cover t Q1294, bl Q831, bm Q108354, br BU10500; title page main MH 12968, bg STT7640; pp 4-5 bg Q58198, p4 MH7739, p5 Q65800; pp 6-7 bg Q70443, p6 Q70236, Q23801; p8 Q564, p9t Q917, 9b Q831; pp10-11 bg Q7269, p 10 Q1294, p11 Q6460; p12 Q23858, p13t Q23873, p13b Q23959; pp14-15bg Q65799Q, p14 Q65802, p15 Q65800; p16 Q108354, p17 Q58198; pp18-19bg B6308, p18 B6004, p19t B10383, p19b B12607; pp20-21bg MH7826, p20t STT7640, p20b MH7739, p21t E7049, p21b MH7759; pp22-23bg MH12991, p22 MH12966, p23 MH12968; pp24-25bg EA73801, p24 EA73796, p25t EA73786, p25b EA73849; pp26-27bg MH862, p26 MH869, p27 MH861; p 28 CL3407, p29 BU10500; p30-31bg MH7826.

Contents

Introduction

Artillery is the class of heavyweight guns that are pulled by horses or armored vehicles, as opposed to light guns, such as rifles or machine guns, that can be carried by hand.

Classification

There are two main types of artillery: guns, which fire high-speed shells at a lower trajectory (flight path), and howitzers, which lob heavier, slower shells at a higher trajectory. Artillery is described by its weight: field or light, medium or heavy. Field or light guns can be towed from place to place. Heavy guns are difficult to move, need assembling in position, and are slow to fire.

Types of Shell

There are many types of shells fired by artillery. High-explosive shells are packed with explosives; they blow up when they hit their target. A shrapnel shell is packed with shrapnel, usually metal balls, and has a bursting charge that explodes in flight, showering the enemy with metal. Armor-piercing shells have a dense core to penetrate the armor of enemy tanks.

Caliber

Artillery is also classified by the internal caliber of its gun barrel: a 75-mm gun has a caliber of 75 mm. Confusingly, different countries employ different systems. The Germans and French have always used metric measurements. The British and Americans used to use imperial measurements, but now use metric. Even more confusingly, the British have also described their artillery by the weight of its shell, so a 60 pounder medium howitzer was fighting alongside a 9.2-inch heavy howitzer during World War I.

All the artillery in this book saw action in either World War I (1914–18) or World War II (1939–45).

Model 1897 75 mm
Field Gun

The French 75, as it was commonly called, was the most famous field gun of World War I. The gun was designed between 1891 and 1896 and went into production in 1897.

Long Service

By the outbreak of war in 1914, more than 4,000 French 75s were in service. The French continued to use this model until the fall of France to the Germans in 1940, ten months after the start of World War II.

SPECS & STATS

Crew	six
Total weight	2,620 lb (1,190 kg)
Barrel length	8.9 ft (2.72 m)
Carriage	six horses or artillery tractor

▼ The versatile "75" was even used as a mobile antiaircraft gun. Mounted on a truck, it was easily movable.

★ The gun's hydro-pneumatic recoil mechanism and wheel brakes kept it stable when firing, which meant the gun did not have to be repositioned before it fired the next shell. It thus achieved a rapid and accurate rate of fire.

★ The quick-acting breech mechanism (for reloading) meant the gun could fire more than 20 shells a minute.

▲ *This French 75 was well camouflaged to hide it from enemy gunners.*

Battle Triumphs

The light and mobile French 75 distinguished itself in two main battles. At the Battle of the Marne in 1914, it helped stop the invading German army from reaching Paris. Two years later, during the lengthy battle for the city of Verdun in 1916, 1,000 French 75s were in action day and night, firing more than 16 million shells. However, although the gun was good against infantry, it was not powerful enough against heavily fortified positions, and it was gradually replaced by heavier field artillery.

ARMAMENTS

Caliber	3 in (75 mm)
Weight and type of shell	11.7-lb (5.2-kg) high-explosive shell
	16-lb (7.2-kg) shrapnel shell
Muzzle velocity	1,735 ft/second (529 m/second)
Range	9,850 yd (9,000 m)
Rate of fire	15–30 rounds/minute

60 pounder Mk I
Medium Howitzer

The 60 pounder (pdr) was the main medium howitzer used by the British during World War I.

It was most effective at knocking out enemy batteries, as it had a long range and fired its heavy shells with great accuracy. However, its rate of fire (two rounds per minute) was slow.

▼ *The gun crew stood well back when firing took place.*

FACT FILE

★ An Mk II version, built in 1918, was more powerful but also 2,200 lb (1,000 kg) heavier. This meant that it could only be towed by a caterpillar tractor or maneuvered on fixed rails.

Crew Eight
Total weight 4.9 tons (4.5 t)
Barrel length 14 ft (4.3 m)
Carriage Twelve horses

Service History

The 60 pounder Mk I was designed in 1904 and saw extensive service on the Western Front during World War I. Both this and the Mk II version continued in service with the British Army into World War II, the last ones seeing action in North Africa between 1940 and 1943.

▲ *A team of horses was required to move a 60 pounder into position.*

▼ *A battery of 60 pounders in position on the Western Front.*

ARMAMENTS

Caliber   5 in (12.7 cm)
Weight and type of shell   60-lb (27-kg) high explosive, shrapnel or gas
Muzzle velocity   2,080 ft/sec (640 m/second)
Range   12,300 yd (11,353 m)
Rate of fire   2 rounds/minute

9.2 in Mk I
Heavy Siege Howitzer

The British 9.2 inch (in) heavy siege howitzer came into service in July 1914, just in time for the outbreak of World War I.

British Expeditionary Force

One of these large guns went across to France in August with the British Expeditionary Force, but it did not see any action until March 1915.

▼ *The crew of the howitzer prepares it for action.*

SPECS & STATS

Weight of gun	16.8 tons (15.2 t)
Carriage	Three trucks drawn by traction engines or teams of horses

Jumping Gun

The gun was not designed for mobility, and it took 36 hours to assemble or dismantle. Because the gun had a short barrel, it had a tendency to jump when fired. This problem was solved by bolting a box filled with 10 tons (9.2 t) of earth onto the front of the gun platform.

ARMAMENTS

Caliber	9.2 in (23.4 cm)
Weight and type of shell	290-lb (132-kg) high explosive
Muzzle velocity	1,197 ft/second (368 m/second)
Range	10,060 yd (9,286 m)

▼ *Camouflage netting hid the howitzer and its shells.*

FACT FILE

★ The 9.2 in Mk I was originally designed as a siege artillery gun to attack fortresses.

★ The Mk II version, which appeared in 1917, had a longer range of 13,935 yd (12,750 m). This version required an extra 9.2 tons (8 t) of earth in the box to keep it steady.

The "Long Max"

The "Long Max" was a German 15 inch (38 cm) SKL/45 naval gun that was adapted during World War I for use on land.

Transporting the Gun

The gun traveled to its destination by railroad and then was mounted on a turntable in a concrete pit. A steel girder construction built across the pit acted as a mount so the gun pointed upward at the correct angle. A narrow-gauge train transported its large shells.

▼ *This "Long Max" is well camouflaged to hide it from the enemy.*

SPECS & STATS

Weight of gun 81 tons (73.5 t)
Barrel length 56 ft (17.1 m)
Carriage Railroad, then mounted on a turntable in a concrete pit

ARMAMENTS

Caliber	15 in (38 cm)
Weight of shell	1,650 lb (750 kg)
Muzzle velocity	3,412 ft/second (1,040 m/second)
Range	29.7 miles (47.5 km)
Rate of fire	2.5 rounds/minute

▶ *Seen from the rear, the "Long Max" was a vast and complex gun.*

◀ *The "Long Max" is loaded for action.*

Long-Range Gun

The Germans used this gun for long-distance shelling of towns and airfields. They installed the first one in eastern France during February 1916 to shell Verdun and its surrounding forts. While these large guns were effective, they were difficult to move around and get ready to fire. As a result, few came into service.

The "Paris Gun"

At 7:18 am on March 21, 1918, a high-explosive shell landed in Paris.

It had been fired by the Germans from the forest of Courcy, 75 miles (120 km) away, and arrived so quietly that the Parisians thought they had been bombarded by a silent airship. The gun that fired this shell was known as the "Paris Gun," and its purpose was to bombard Paris.

Long Range

The gun is considered by some historians to have been a terror weapon built by Germany to demoralize the French. Because the gun had such a long range, its gunners had to take into account the rotation of the Earth when calculating where its shells would land.

FACT FILE

★ Each shell fired by the "Paris Gun" reached almost five times the speed of sound and reached up into the stratosphere, higher than any other human missile in history until the first successful V-2 test flight in October 1942 (*see* pages 28–29).

Assembling the "Paris Gun" at its testing site in Germany.

Caliber	8.3 in (21 cm)
Weight and type of shell	210-lb (94-kg) high explosive shell
Muzzle velocity	5,200 ft/sec (1,600 m/sec)
Range	80 miles (130 km) in 170 seconds at max altitude of 24 miles (40 km)
Rate of fire	1 round/3 minutes

SPECS & STATS

Crew	Eighty German naval gunners commanded by an admiral
Weight of gun	282 tons (256 t)
Barrel length	92 ft (28 m) with a 20 ft (6 m) smooth bore extension
Carriage	Rotating mount

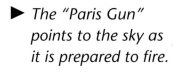

▶ *The "Paris Gun" points to the sky as it is prepared to fire.*

M.G.3c.

Design Faults

The Paris Gun's accuracy was not that good: gunners could hit Paris, but not a specific target in the city. The gun was also not that effective, as each shell was fired at such a high speed that it wore away the bore of the gun. After 65 shells had been fired—each one slightly bigger to fit the ever-widening bore—the barrel had to be re-bored.

520 mm Schneider Howitzer

The French 520 mm Schneider howitzer holds first place in the record books for firing the biggest shells of World War I.

Each shell was 3,130 lb (1,420 kg) in weight and 20.5 in (520 mm) in diameter. The shells were designed to penetrate their target before exploding. The gun came into service in May 1918, but saw little action before the war ended that November.

ARMAMENTS

Caliber	20.5 in (520 mm)
Weight of shell	3,130 lb (1,420 kg)
Range	10 miles (16 km)

▼ *The angle of the howitzer's barrel could be altered up or down but not traversed side to side.*

P. 3013

Mounted on Rails

The 520 mm Schneider was fixed onto a railway carriage just under 100 ft (30 m) long which weighed almost 331 tons (300 t). Because it could not traverse, the carriage was towed round a curved siding so that its gun was pointing in the right direction. When it was fired, the recoil was so great that the carriage rolled back down the track.

▼ *Firing the howitzer on its carriage.*

Bofors 40 mm
Light Antiaircraft Gun

In 1928, the Swedish navy ordered the development of a new 1.6-inch (40-mm) naval antiaircraft gun from the Bofors company.

The gun proved to be light, fast, and reliable. A ground-based version on a four-wheeled carriage was soon developed. Seventeen different nations bought the model, and it became the most widely used antiaircraft gun of World War II.

British Usage

The British army adopted the gun in 1937. Its accuracy and rate of fire were particularly effective against low-flying or dive-bombing aircraft.

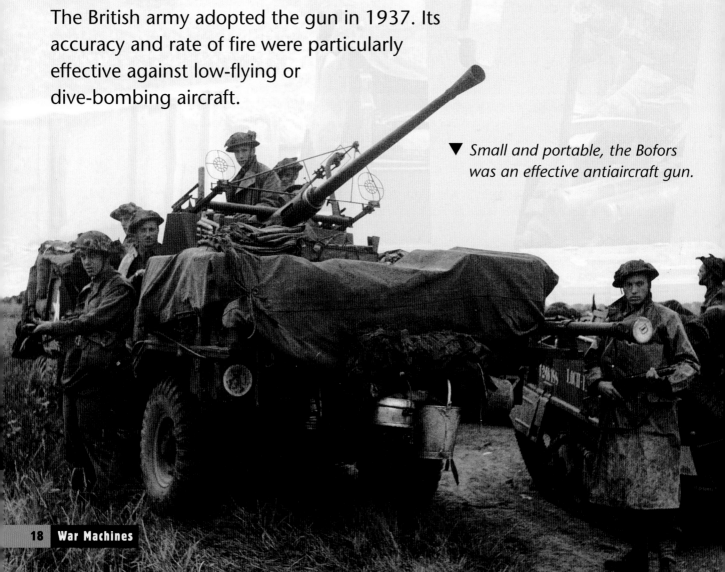

▼ *Small and portable, the Bofors was an effective antiaircraft gun.*

A number of versions were also developed for the Royal Navy. The gun was so successful that it remained in service with the British army until the 1980s.

FACT FILE

★ The Bofors gun could be fired from its carriage with no setup required, although it was not always that accurate. If the gunners had time, they could use the tow-bar and muzzle lock as levers to raise the wheels off the ground and lower the gun onto supporting pads. Two additional legs folded out on either side. This could be done in less than a minute.

▲ *The crew of a Bofors gun guards bridges across the Rhine in the last months of World War II.*

SPECS & STATS

Crew	Six
Total weight	4,367 lb (1,981 kg)
Barrel length	7.5 ft (2.24 m)
Carriage	Four-wheeled towable carriage

ARMAMENTS

Caliber	1.6 in (40 mm)
Weight and type of shell	2 lb (.9 kg) high explosive
Maximum ceiling	23,600 ft (7,193 m)
Muzzle velocity	2,890 ft/second (881 m/second)
Range	23,500 ft (7,160 m)
Rate of fire	120 rounds/minute

▶ *A gunner finds time to write a Christmas card home.*

5 cm PaK 38
Antitank Gun

▲ *The 5 cm PaK 38 is in the center, with its successor, the larger 7.5 cm PaK 40, on the left and its predecessor, the smaller 3.7 cm PaK 36, on the right.*

The German 5 cm PaK 38 antitank gun was developed in 1938 and entered service in April 1940.

Tungsten Shells

When the German army attacked the Soviet Union (USSR) in 1941, they used the PaK 38 gun to fire armor-piercing (AP) shells with a core of tungsten, a very hard, heavy metal, at Soviet tanks. These tungsten-cored shells could penetrate 3.4 in (8.6 cm) into armor at a range of around 1,500 ft (470 m), making the gun highly effective against most tanks. After the supply of tungsten ran out in 1942, the gun's effectiveness using other shells dropped considerably.

◄ *This side view of the gun shows its lightweight construction.*

The low silhouette of the gun made it easy to conceal, which was especially important when fighting in the exposed Western Desert of North Africa.

▲ *British gunners load a shell into a captured PaK.*

FACT FILE

★ PaK stands for *Panzerabwehrkanone*, the German word for "antitank cannon."

★ The PaK 38 had solid rubber tires that needed little maintenance and conserved rubber, a scarce commodity in Germany during the war.

SPECS & STATS

Crew	Six
Total weight	2,174 lb (986 kg)
Barrel length	9.85 ft (3 m)
Carriage	Split-trail (two-pronged) carriage on two wheels

ARMAMENTS

Caliber	1.97 in (5 cm)
Weight and type of shell	6.2 lb (2.8 kg) AP shell
Muzzle velocity	2,740 ft/second (835 m/second)
Range	9,000 ft (2,745 m)
Rate of fire	13 rounds/minute

◀ *A close-up of the breech.*

5.5 in Mk III
Medium Gun

The British 5.5 inch (in) medium gun first entered service in the Western Desert in North Africa against the Germans and the Italians in May 1942.

Its carriage and breech mechanisms were not adequate at first, and it had a disappointing range. However, various design changes and a lighter shell soon made it highly effective.

Long Service

The Mk III gun soon became one of the most effective guns in the British army and saw action in almost every theater of war. It remained in service until 1978.

The split-tail carriage of the gun is opened out to stabilize it during firing. Note the open breech.

Caliber	5.5 in (14 cm)
Weight and type of shell	100-lb (45.5-kg) high-explosive shell, later reduced to a 80-lb (36-kg) shell
Muzzle velocity	1,700 ft/second (517 m/second)
Range	8.7 miles (14 km) for a 100 lb (45.5 kg) shell
Rate of fire	3 rounds/minute

A view of the gun with the breech closed.

FACT FILE

★ Between June 1944 and May 1945, the 21st Army Group in northwest Europe fired 2,610,747 rounds of shells using 5.5 in Mk III guns.

SPECS & STATS

Crew	Nine
Total weight	13,669 lb (6,200 kg)
Barrel length	13.8 ft (4.2 m)
Carriage	AEC Matador artillery tractor

M1 155 mm Howitzer

The M1 155 mm towed howitzer entered service with the United States (U.S.) Army in 1942 and continued to be used through both the Korean War of the 1950s and the Vietnam War of the 1960s.

It was withdrawn from U.S. service in 1982, although it remains in use today in at least 40 countries.

▼ *In action in northern France after the Allied invasion of Europe in June 1944*

▲ A crew shelters the howitzer under a tree to hide it from enemy guns.

1944

The M1 saw most action after D-Day and the invasion of western Europe in June 1944. It was used during the capture of Cherbourg in late June and the subsequent battle for Normandy in July and August 1944.

SPECS & STATS

Crew	Eleven
Total weight	12,346 lb (5,600 kg)
Barrel length	12.4 ft (3.78 m)
Carriage	Split-trail (two-pronged) carriage on two wheels

▶ A close-up of the breech

ARMAMENTS

Caliber	6.1 in (155 mm)
Type of shell	High explosive
Muzzle velocity	1,850 ft/second (569 m/second)
Range	9.2 miles (14.6 km)
Rate of fire	40 rounds/hour

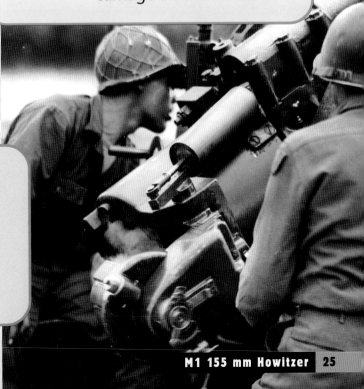

80 cm K (E) "Schwere Gustav" Gun

The German "Schwere Gustav" (meaning "Heavy Gustav") gun was possibly the largest gun ever built.

It was so big that it took 25 trainloads of equipment, 1,400 men, and up to six weeks to assemble. Yet it was only used for 13 days and fired a total of 48 shells.

FACT FILE

★ Two of these massive railway guns were built. The first was named "Gustav" after Gustav Geschutz, an engineer at the Krupp works where it was built. The second was named "Dora" after his wife.

★ The gun was transported by rail in kit form and assembled on site, ready for firing.

◀ The "Gustav" was so big its carriage sat on parallel sets of rails.

Crew	1,420 men commanded by a colonel, including 500 gunners
Weight of gun	1,505 tons (1,366 t)
Barrel length	164 ft (50 m)
Carriage	Railway truck

Attack on Sevastopol

This massive gun was originally designed to smash the Maginot Line of defensive forts that protected France's eastern border with Germany. However the gun was not ready in time for the attack in May 1940. In June 1942 it traveled along railway tracks across Europe and was installed in the Crimea, ready to attack the Soviet Black Sea port of Sevastopol. The gun proved to be a great success, easily demolishing heavily protected Soviet coastal batteries, fortresses, and ammunition magazines.

▼ *The "Gustav" was a great success in the Crimea, but when that battle was over, it was dismantled and taken back to Germany, never to fire a shell again.*

ARMAMENTS

Caliber	31.5 in (80 cm)
Weight and type of shell	16,540-lb (7,460-kg) concrete-piercing shell
	10,584-lb (4,800-kg) high-explosive shell
Muzzle velocity	2,500 ft/second (760 m/second)
Range	23 miles (37 km) for concrete-piercing shell
	30 miles (48 km) for high-explosive shell
Rate of fire	14 rounds/day

V-2 Rocket

The German V-2 rocket was the first man-made object ever to be sent into space and is thus the forerunner of modern space rockets.

How It Worked

The V-2 consisted of a large warhead sitting on top of a powerful rocket engine that launched it up into space. After a minute, the engine cut out and the rocket flew through space before returning to Earth and hitting its target four minutes later, causing widespread death and devastation. Its flight path was controlled by an internal accelerometer that cut the engine off at the right time, thus dictating how far the rocket would fly.

Rocket Trials

The first V-2 test launch took place in March 1942, but the rocket crash-landed nearby. The third test rocket was launched successfully on October 3, 1942. It flew for 120 miles (193 km) and reached a height of 50 miles (80 km), the first rocket ever to reach space. On September 8, 1944, V-2s attacked Paris and London.

▶ *An engineer makes adjustments to the gyroscopes that will control its stability and distance in flight.*

SPECS & STATS

Total weight 14.1tons (12.8 t)

Height 47 ft (14.3 m)

Speed 4,400 ft/second (1,340 m/second)

Altitude 56 miles (90 km)

Engine Liquid-fueled rocket engine combining 8,378 lb (3,800 kg) of fuel (75% alcohol, 25% water) with 10,802 lb (4,900 kg) of liquid oxygen

Thrust 55,000 lb (24,950 kg) at the start, increasing to 160,000 lb (72,570 kg) at maximum speed

▼ *A V-2 stands against its gantry ready for launch.*

FACT FILE

★ Because the V-2 traveled for most of its journey without power, it arrived at its target silently. Civilians had no warning that they were about to be attacked.

ARMAMENTS

Warhead 2,200 lb (1,000 kg) of amatol, a high explosive made of TNT and ammonium nitrate

Range 185 miles (300 km)

Glossary

Antiaircraft gun
A gun designed to hit enemy aircraft and bring them down.

Antitank gun
A powerful gun designed to pierce armor and "kill" or knock out an enemy tank.

AP
Armor-piercing shell.

Artillery
Heavy guns pulled by horses or armored vehicles. It can also refer to the section of the army firing the weapons.

Barrel
The long tube through which the shell is fired.

Battery
A unit of typically 6 to 8 artillery guns, grouped together to help battlefield communications and command; batteries are grouped in larger units called battalions, which are further grouped into regiments.

Breech
The opening at the end or side of the gun barrel through which the shell is inserted.

Caliber
The diameter of the bore or the inside of the barrel of a gun.

Carriage
The method by which the artillery piece is moved.

Field gun
Lightweight gun, with a bore-diameter up to about 6 in (15 cm).

Gun
Artillery designed to fire a high-velocity shell at a low trajectory or flight path.

Heavy gun
A heavyweight gun with a bore diameter above 8 in (20 cm).

Howitzer
Artillery designed to fire a heavy, slower shell with a high trajectory or flight path.

hp
Horsepower, a unit of power.

Medium gun
A medium-weight gun, with a bore diameter between 6 and 8 in (15-20 cm).

Mk
Short for Mark, the model or type of gun.

Muzzle velocity
The rate per second at which a shell exits the muzzle of the gun.

pdr
Short for "pounder."

Rate of fire
The number of shells that can be fired in a period of time.

Recoil
When a gun jumps or rolls back as a result of being fired.

Shell
A hollow artillery projectile filled with either high explosives or shrapnel and primed with a fuse to explode either during flight, on impact, or after penetration.

Shrapnel
Small pieces of metal, often metal balls, packed into a shell and designed as an anti-personnel weapon to kill or maim the enemy.

Supersonic
Flight greater than the speed of sound, which is 769 miles (1238 km) per hour at 70°F.

Western Front
The parallel line of Allied and German trenches that ran from the English Channel south through Belgium and France to the Swiss border, and where most of the major battles of World War I took place.

Useful Web Sites

First World War.com—Vintage Photographs—Artillery
http://www.firstworldwar.com/photos/artillery.htm

The Imperial War Museum
http://www.iwm.org.uk/

Trenches on the Web—Photo Archive: Big Guns of the Great War
http://www.worldwar1.com/pharc005.htm

Sites about the two World Wars:

The Great War (World War I) from PBS
www.pbs.org/greatwar/

The Perilous Fight: America's World War II in Color
www.pbs.org/perilousfight/battlefield/

BBC history sites about the two world wars:
www.bbc.co.uk/history/worldwars/wwone/
www.bbc.co.uk/history/worldwars/wwtwo/

Index